INJUSTICE

WRONGFULLY CONVICTED and WRONFULLY ACCUSSED

The path to the truth may need further verification.

Author: Dana M. Way

Preface: Jonathon P. Helsius

Edited: Eula M. B. Turner

⁂

Preface

Diverse individuals within the criminal justice system are responsible for ensuring that "justice is blind". Typically, the process begins with a crime being committed and a victim identified. The victim must be willing to report the crime and should be deemed competent and truthful. The law enforcement agency that has jurisdiction over the crime site starts the investigation. This jurisdiction can be shared by a Police Department, a County Sheriff's Office, a state investigative agency or a federal investigative agency. Usually, one law enforcement agency takes the lead in investigating the alleged criminal activity.

The success of any investigation depends on the skills, training, experience, and professionalism of the law enforcement officers carrying out a systematic inquiry to discover and examine the facts. Each officer takes an oath to uphold the law and to enforce the law without prejudice.

Each officer is bound by a code of ethics, the guide for proper conduct and impartiality. Each officer is held to a high standard of conduct, and any intentional wrong doing, usually, results in swift sanctions and, in some cases, dismissal and criminal charges. The "public trust" in law enforcement officers is cherished by most of those who wear the badge.

An investigation usually starts with the officer on the street, but the successful prosecution of a criminal goes way beyond "the cop on the beat". When a suspect is identified, the process of looking closely at or eliminating that individual from consideration begins. A good investigator looks at four basic elements to evaluate a suspect: opportunity, capability, intent, and motive.

Professionally trained officers gather evidence. The result is usually a mound of forensic results and piles of lab reports. The district attorney (DA) or prosecutor reviews criminal cases and decides whether a suspected criminal should be indicted. The DA's decision is based on the presentation and merits of the evidence. In the more serious criminal cases, the DA convenes a grand jury who listens to the probable cause testimony and may issue an indictment. The investigative and decision-making processes, however, are not foolproof!

Sometimes, even though there are real issues in proving guilt, the investigator moves forward, convinced that the right guy was accused. Occasionally, evidence that might prove the suspect's innocence is withheld from the defense attorney.

Forensic technicians, evidence custodians, medical examiners, and crime lab scientists, to name a few, each play a part in bringing a criminal to justice. Even though one person's failure can cause an innocent person to be convicted because of tainted or misrepresented evidence, "spot on work" by all can ensure the integrity of an investigation and punishment for the guilty person.

A criminal charge may be dismissed before it reaches the courtroom if the physical evidence is not appropriate or if an officer made a procedural mistake. Perhaps the confession wasn't constitutionally sound. Or maybe evidence was seized without legal justification. The prosecutor acts as a check to balance the actions of the law enforcement officer and/or investigator.

When the case goes to court, the defendant appears before a judge and enters a plea of guilty or not guilty. During the investigation, however, he should be presumed innocent. In most cases, a lengthy process of plea negotiations takes place between the DA and the defense attorney. The defense attorney has a right to view the evidence the prosecution plans to present. If the evidence is substantial, it may be wise for the defendant to plead guilty to a lesser offense and, perhaps, spend less time in the "slammer". In court, however, the prosecutor must prove, beyond a reasonable doubt, that the accused person is guilty of the crime.

But, what if the person is innocent? Are innocent people really charged with crimes and convicted?

Yes, it does happen. Occasionally, there are problems with criminal prosecutions. The "checks and balances" designed to protect the innocent sometimes fail, mainly due to human error. Human beings are flawed, and most of us have heard the phrase, "To err is human; to forgive, divine."

Personal beliefs and values, prejudices, and the desire to put a bad person behind bars may affect the outcome of an investigation. Attitudes like "The end justifies the means" or an investigator's 100% conviction of a suspect's guilt may also undermine justice and affect many lives. Yet, not all criminal investigations are riddled with deceit. Most people working in the criminal justice arena are highly ethical and professional.

The criminal justice system, however, is not very forgiving. A mistake made by anyone, at any time during the investigative process may result in a miscarriage of justice. Whether the mistake is innocent (lack of training or experience, understaffing or overwhelm) or purposeful and unethical, usually it negatively affects the outcome of the investigation.

Despite our constitutional right to be represented by legal counsel and our right to prepare a defense and have experts testify on our behalf, the system does not always work perfectly.

I've investigated a lot of serious crimes in my almost 30 years of wearing the badge. Some crime scenes are still etched into my memory. I've seen horrible people do horrible things to other people. I had to find those people and bring them to justice while working within the confines of the law. I wasn't always successful, and sometimes murderers were not prosecuted.

Yet, nothing brought me more satisfaction than the hard work and tenacious attitude that allowed me to arrest someone who had committed a heinous crime. I thought that all law enforcement officers were like me. Looking back, I think most of them were, but what about the ones who weren't?

Before becoming familiar with the Dana Way's work, I was skeptical of the value of defense experts. I saw them as the enemy who wanted to discredit me and my work and let guilty people off the hook. Now I have seen how some lazy, careless and/or incompetent investigators rush to judgment and botch investigations. I learned that an innocent person could not only be accused of a crime but also convicted and imprisoned.

Knowing the citizens keep a critical eye on people like me makes me a better officer and investigator. As a law enforcement officer, the greatest disservice I can do is put the wrong person in prison. Shedding light on some of the mistakes made within the criminal justice system can make

positive change probable.

Dana Way wrote this book to make people aware of

injustices within the justice system. She also seeks to

provide hope to the individuals and families who face daily

obstacles because of a wrongful conviction.

FOREWORD

The stories in this book are based on real incidents. The names and places have been changed to protect the privacy of the people involved.

Today we live in a world where injustice is present for many reasons. Maybe the police officers have been collecting evidence for a trial but have had trouble substantiating the evidence necessary for an arrest. Racial bias is also a factor. Sometimes a department needs better focused investigations or more effective recordkeeping to resolve cases.

Whatever the reason, whatever the fundamental issue, the truth cannot be forced. A conviction must be based on accumulated evidence, and the accusations must be solidly founded from both sides of the courtroom.

Lady Justice is blind. Or is she? Fair is fair in the courtroom,

right? Not exactly! As a consultant for the defense counsel, I

do not have the same laboratory training that federal or

local government agents have had in this field.

Consequently, I have had to endure hours of questioning in

Daubert Hearings.

Daubert Hearings are required when the defense counsel

attempts to introduce a witness as an expert who can offer

valuable testimony in the case but who may not be clearly

qualified by education or training in a particular field of

study. Only a judge can render a decision as to whether a

witness is an expert or not. Unfortunately, with the same

information, different judges in different courtrooms render

different decisions.

I was disqualified in only two cases; this meant that I was

not allowed to testify because the judge did not accept my

credentials. The facts of both of these cases will be related

in this book. In both cases, my testimony may have shed a

different light on the facts presented to the jury and may not have led to a conviction.

Some judges demand credibility for the defense witnesses from outside training. The witness must be twice as good and have done twice as much BECAUSE the training offered to the state and federal government IS NOT available to those not employed by such agencies. I am not saying that the training offered by such agencies isn't worthwhile or is short in duration. In fact the training is very intense, and agency personnel must undergo several hours of in-service training to maintain their standing and certifications. The consultant for the defense counsel, however, must match or, in some cases, do more. Yet, even that may not be enough!

What did I do? I graduated from Virginia Commonwealth University with a Bachelor of Science degree from the school of Education with a concentration in Chemistry. Back in 1988, this is how things were done if you wanted the option to ever teach. I have 32 credit hours of Chemistry

should I ever want to enroll in a graduate program in

chemistry. I spent one year as a Chemist at Commonwealth

Laboratories, a small laboratory in Richmond, VA. I ran

mostly environmental samples and had some time to work

with Blood Alcohols on a Gas Chromatograph. My best

friend was in charge, and he taught me how to analyze the

samples. In the next laboratory, my main responsibility was

for toxic metals.

After it was discovered that this lab was responsible for

dumping contaminated product into the monitoring wells, I

sought employment with Roche Analytics Laboratories in

Richmond, VA. Here I concentrated on industrial hygiene

and again focused on toxic metals. I received further

education and knowledge and more instrumentation at this

laboratory. I spent the next 5 years of my Chemistry career

at Roche Analytics Laboratories.

In a laboratory, identification of a substance always begins by looking at a known substance and then doing a comparison to an unknown substance to see if there is a distinction. For example, an apple is an apple based on its properties, but some may look slightly different than others. Some are green, some are pink, some are dark red, and some even come with slightly different shapes, but they are all apples. Chemical identification can be thought of similarly in some cases. If an unknown chemical reacts similarly to the known standard and appears to have the same properties, then it is presumed that the unknown is of the same constitute or composition as the known.

While it is impossible to enlighten you on all aspects of how chemistry works or even how it is used in all cases in just one book. What I have presented is a simplified overview so that the cases can be better understood.

Not all chemical analyses is as simple as chemical identification, and deoxyribonucleic acid (DNA), a self-replicating material present in nearly all living organisms and the carrier of genetic information, is not simple at all. Even though DNA is extremely complicated, it presents a comparison style of identification.

The history of forensic science dates to the year 700; early forensic scientists were self-taught. It was not a discipline in colleges and universities in the United States until around 1950 when the University of Berkeley established the first academic departments of criminology and criminalistics. The American Academy of Forensic Science (AAFS) was formed in Chicago during that same year.

Advances were made in forensic science during almost every year of the 19th Century, and several firsts were documented during the 1980s. Since then, forensic science has made regular strides and yielded more clear and concise recognition patterns using more sensitive instrumentation, better practices and procedures, and constant levels of validation studies. Each laboratory is responsible for validating its own practices and procedures and are all monitored and governed by some higher authority; i.e., The American Society of Crime Laboratory Directors (ASCLD).

After college and a six-year run in the laboratory, I discovered a means of self-employment. I built electronic components for laboratory analytical equipment in addition to robotics, defense communication systems, emergency response equipment, and more. Being a chemist got me into the small world of analytical equipment because I not only understood the instrumentation but also the environment in which the instruments were placed.

After seven years in this business, a friend of mine, a former probation officer, recommended that I use my knowledge of chemistry to consult for defense attorneys. "Both sides should have equal representation," she explained. She mentioned that the work would be satisfying.

I thought she was crazy! I didn't think that anyone would give me a second thought. However, to satisfy both my curiosity and her insistence, I sent out some inquiries. Was I in for a surprise! I got several calls almost immediately. I never imagined what was getting ready to unfold.

INTRODUCTION: *The Truth Seeker*

As a young girl, my interest in the criminal justice system was always high. Most of the books I read were based on some level of "who done it". True crime stories were my absolute favorite.

Growing up, I aspired to be part of the esteemed group that presented the real truth to the world and put away the bad guys. In my day, we had few mystery or crime solving TV programs. In my spare time, I was in my room reading the likes of Nancy Drew, The Hardy Boys, and anything regarding crimes I could find.

The science and the investigation were most fascinating. The steps the investigators took with such passion to make sure the right person got discovered, arrested, and convicted was what drove me to want to be like them when I grew up.

As life would have it, sometimes our course of action gets slightly adjusted based on other influences, such as family and evolving goals. Mine eventually evolved to turn toward the sciences because it was the unseen facts that intrigued me the most. Discovering the truths within science was far more rewarding, and I could help so many more people. Teaching others science was a more impactful path, and it greatly satisfied my parents too. They would not have been at all thrilled to have discovered my true interests in law enforcement.

I never mentioned it to them because I knew what I would have endured in the conversations surrounding the topic. My father would have likely pointed out that it was a thankless job, that little or no gratitude would be given, and that the money was horrible, not to mention the hours! My mother would have pointed out the dangers and would have likely taken great pains to point out some more positive, safer careers for me.

At the end of the day I would have done what I wanted to anyway, but the chemistry was truly intriguing. By the time I was seriously entertaining the idea of going into law enforcement and contemplating working with the DEA (Drug Enforcement Agency) as my end goal, I was married.

And when I presented it to my husband, he responded quickly, "I will divorce you if you choose this path!"

I had no idea why at the time, but I was slightly weakened with emotion for him and our 6 month-old baby boy. So I eliminated the thought from my mind and stayed in the lab discovering truths in the Industrial Hygiene world. I was keeping workers safe from harmful work environments.

Because I had never been in trouble or really knew anyone who had been in trouble, it wasn't until the O.J. Simpson case that anything akin to fabricating a situation was ever a question in my mind as it related to law enforcement and the justice system. During the Simpson case, however, I was amazed at the lengths people went to create the perfect situation to achieve an outcome favorable to one side or another. Did this happen just to high profile people or was this kind of thing happening to others less fortunate that no one knew anything about?

At that moment of realization, I shook my head and thought, "I hope this isn't a consistent happening … getting something to appear the way the prosecution wants it to."

More than ten years later, my dear friend convinced me to reconsider some conversations we had previously. She has a mocha complexion and is grouped ethnically as an African American. Several ethnicities exist in her DNA, from Spanish to Native American. In her lifetime, she has seen the trials and tribulations of the injustices of the justice system first hand, first as a probation officer and then later as a substance abuse counselor and now a clinical director.

Reflecting on the conversation now, I can see that she was nearly begging me to step forward and work this field because she knew me well enough after 5 or 6 years to know that I was a truth seeker. I would not bend for anything or anybody. I simply cared about the truth and presenting it, not about how many convictions were needed or who was up for election or whose political back needed to be scratched.

The very first case I worked was an eye opener where the difference between trafficking and possession of heroin meant loss of all assets to the government and more time in prison and therefore more assets for the government. So how or why would anyone question a crime lab report of 4.2 grams, only 0.3 grams over the amount needed to seize everything the defendant owned and the assurance of many more years in prison? The "how" came with me, but it's still a mystery as to how almost a half a gram of heroin disappeared when only a tenth of a gram was necessary for testing. Maybe, just maybe, it wasn't there to begin with.

⸮

CHAPTER ONE: How much does that heroin

really weigh?

The first call and the first case for 3rd Degree Investigations Inc. came from Attorney Larry McDonald, a criminal attorney in Raleigh, NC. I was shocked that I got a response so quickly.

"Hey, I have this client here that has been arrested on a trafficking charge for Heroin," said Attorney McDonald. "The crime lab weighed it at 4.2 grams, and my client would like to get it re-weighed. Is this something you can do?"

At this point, I had to use an outside crime lab because I had no tools of the trade in my office. The only lab I trusted and that had the necessary DEA license to handle narcotics was a lab in Pennsylvania. So I would have to use Federal Express (FEDEX) to get the sample to Pennsylvania. FEDEX is considered the only secure transporter of evidence.

After receiving the court order issued by the judge and delivered to me by the attorney, I took the order along with the label for transport to the evidence department of the Raleigh Police Department. The evidence custodian and the arresting officer packaged the evidence and placed the label on the sealed box. The box was then taken to the area where shipping and receiving are handled and sent off to the lab in Pennsylvania. The chain of custody was not broken, and no unauthorized person had handled the evidence.

Once the evidence arrived at the lab in Pennsylvania, the chain of custody remained intact with the first signature of the Fed Ex package. The evidence was reweighed, and the total weight was 3.8 grams, four tenths of a gram under the trafficking level of 4.2 grams.

I called Attorney McDonald, "We got the results back on the reweigh; the heroin weighed only 3.8 grams."

Larry asked, "How can such a difference be explained? Would they have used four tenths of a gram in testing at the crime lab?"

"Not typically," I answered. "Most of the time, the loss for or during analysis is only about a tenth of a gram."

"Well then," said Larry, "would it be fair to say that perhaps the 4.2 gram initial weight may not have been totally accurate?"

"It is possible; however, I cannot say that definitively. What I can say is that we now only have 3.8 grams of heroin, and the remaining sample is on its way back to Raleigh evidence. I will have a report for you to present by tomorrow."

"Thank you, I will be looking for it in my email."

I presented the report with the documentation of the chain of custody from the lab and the analyst's lab notes. The charge was reduced to possession with the intent to sell rather than trafficking, and my testimony was not needed in court. I never met this defendant; the only thing I knew of him was that he was charged with more substance than was actually present.

This case was an eye opener, my girlfriend was right as usual. How many more persons accused of a crime in a criminal prosecution were out there like this one? How many cases had been tried that, perhaps, were on the cusp like this one and didn't get a second look?

It was time to purchase an analytical balance with certified weights for the next time. This would prevent having to secure-ship any evidence, thereby, reducing the risk of losing evidence or parts of evidence. The purchase also would allow for immediate observation of both the prosecution and the defense lawyers. It would also ensure that evidence was never out of the possession of the original evidence department of the agency or office. Additionally, I would be ready to go for the next case that needed a second opinion.

Two weeks later my equipment arrived with carrying case

that I could take anywhere. So, it began.

⁇

CHAPTER 2: *75 grams of Crack Cocaine in New Orleans*

The next call came from New Orleans, a well-known attorney whose name was Kevin Matthews. Kevin is a criminal attorney who works with high profile cases in the area, and his client was alleged to have had 75 grams of crack cocaine.

Of the four phone lines in my office, one is dedicated to 3rd Degree Investigations. The other three lines are for the electronics company that manufactures next door to my office. The phone rang, and I answered, "3rd Degree Investigations, this is Dana speaking, how may I help you?"

"Hi Dana, this is Kevin Matthews, an attorney here in New Orleans. I have a client who's has been charged with possession of 75 grams of Crack Cocaine. He wishes to have this evidence reweighed. Is this something you can help with?"

I explained that I absolutely could. "I need to obtain a court order to begin the process, I have my own balance and certified weights, so I can do the reweigh right on site at the evidence location with as many people present as wish to attend. At a minimum, I recommend at least one party from the prosecution and, of course, one member of the defense team other than me. The evidence custodian remains with the evidence as to not break the chain of custody."

"That is great Dana, I will get back to you once I obtain the order."

"I look forward to hearing back from you."

Kevin called a few weeks later, and we arranged a flight with a hotel and the process necessary for the reweigh to occur. I was staying in the hotel adjacent to the United

States Attorney's Office and would need to be on the 4th floor of the office building by 10 am the following morning.

I landed in New Orleans the afternoon before the reweigh and went straight to the hotel. The city can be a scary place for some, and for me it was a little unnerving because 75 grams of Crack Cocaine is nothing to shake a stick at. The client was in quite a bit of trouble, and I wasn't exactly sure how I was going to make a difference.

Yet, I was the only one I knew of who could travel with analytical balance in tow and reweigh evidence. No one else to my knowledge was providing this service. I had noticed some people at the airport who seemed to be lingering in the area where I was, and I noticed the same people at the hotel upon my arrival. Not sure if they were lingering for me or not, but it seemed unusual at the least. I didn't leave my room that night, had food ordered in, and reported to the fourth floor of the adjacent building by 10 am.

I had an evening flight, out so there was no big rush. I had had a cup of coffee, but I was starving. Even though I knew I could eat when this was over, my thoughts kept going to the reason I was here – again 75 grams was a lot of crack.

Kevin and I waited in the front of the US Attorney's Office until the evidence arrived in an interview room for reevaluation. We were called to the interview room when the evidence arrived. After greeting the US Attorney and the arresting officer, I unpacked the balance and allowed the electronics to warm up. The balance takes about ten minutes to warm up, and then the certified weights can be measured. In the meanwhile, I got out my notebook and weights.

The evidence was stored in a sealed manila envelope with identifying markings on it indicating the same item number and case number that were listed on the court order. Inside the manila envelope was a sealed plastic bag containing another sealed plastic bag of the evidence. I inspected the original sealed packaging to make certain we had the right evidence. In this case, it seemed like we might have had a mix up. When the evidence was pulled from the first sealed plastic bag, the smell in the room became overwhelming. It was such a horrible, chemical smell that I could not wait to get away from it.

I glanced at the evidence. Much to my surprise, it looked nothing like Crack Cocaine, and in fact, it didn't even have the consistency of Crack Cocaine. Crack Cocaine is a hard substance ranging in color from pale yellow to pale pink or white. What was in the bag across the table from me was a dark yellow mush. I thought to myself, "What in the Sam Hill do I do with this? – holy crap!"

I asked, "Are we sure that is Crack Cocaine?"

The arresting officer replied, "It is. And we know it to be adulterated with Procaine, a numbing agent sometimes found in Crack Cocaine. We think the Procaine is what has caused it to be like a mush now."

"We can't think. We need to know what has caused this change. Surely this is not the way it was seized. Now we have more than one problem: we have something that used to be Crack Cocaine that may not be in the same form and most definitely may not weigh anywhere close to 75 grams. Are we in agreement – both defense and prosecution – that I should complete the reweigh as I have been called here to do?"

The answer was affirmative.

I reweighed the substance in the bag because it was so slushy that It was easier to reweigh in the first plastic bag. A correction for the plastic bag could be accounted for in my report as most plastic bags weigh less than a tenth of a gram, and this one likely weighed right at a tenth of a gram.

The weight of the substance was only 35.67 grams. That's less than half of the alleged 75 grams!

Most likely, the reduction to slush had much to do with the weight loss, but what caused the change in composition in the first place? That was the question of the day!

I was then asked to determine what might have caused the reduction and if the Procaine could have had anything to do with the loss of product consistency. I agreed to help. Now I am basically working for both sides it seems, and only one side is paying me, the defense team.

I had the pleasure of meeting Kevin's client, Mr. Chad Robinson, a retired veteran. As he sat in his wheelchair, he shook my hand and thanked me for traveling from Raleigh to New Orleans to help him with his case.

It was not for me to question why a retired veteran in a wheel chair would allegedly have any amount of an illicit substance, but I needed to work on the issue at hand – a reduced product that had the chemical makeup of Crack Cocaine. Interesting scenario!

Now I had to go home and figure out what caused the reduction to this Crack Cocaine that we had never seen before. Smart phones weren't quite what they are now, and I did not bring my computer with me. Throughout the trip, home I contemplated causes.

I was certain that Procaine did not possess properties that would cause a reduction reaction, and the mush smelled so bad that the only thing I could think of was perhaps the Crack had been mentholated. Now how to test that theory was yet another quandary. I could not legally possess Cocaine to remanufacture the possible process of mentholated Crack Cocaine. So, what could I do?

I reached out to one of my pharmaceutical clients from the electronics side of my businesses and got some pharmaceutical grade caffeine. Caffeine and cocaine have nearly identical properties so I manufactured "Crack Caffeine". I boiled the caffeine with sodium bicarbonate (baking soda) and used the same drying process. I made some without menthol and some with menthol and I split the samples after they had dried completely (approximately 24 hours later) for frozen storage and room temperature storage.

I discovered that the "Crack Caffeine" without Menthol did not change in weight over four weeks of daily measurements at room temperature or frozen. The "Crack Caffeine" with Menthol, however, was a completely different story. The frozen samples remained a consistent weight form the very first day after the 24-hour drying period. The room temperature samples, however, grew just slightly more than three times the original weight after the drying over the next 36 to 72 hours. Profoundly, the series of weights taken after 72 hours weights continued to be lower and lower each day and eventually turned to a slush rather than a solid.

It was clear that the product I had examined and weighed in New Orleans most likely had a reduction due to the addition of menthol and, while the product was no longer in the form in which it was likely seized, I would still do a report of my findings and send the data I used to come to my conclusions. It was up to the attorneys to sort it out.

My report of the mentholated Crack Cocaine impacted how the product was stored by New Orleans police departments. If an officer suspected the presence of menthol, he would store the cocaine in a freezer. Something to be proud of I suppose – little ol' me writing a report for the US Attorney's Office in New Orleans that made a difference! This is what satisfaction feels like to me. While it may not have had the outcome Mr. Robinson was hoping for, we discovered an alternate and better way handle Crack Cocaine that had been mentholated.

CHAPTER 3: *Louden County – Marijuana, cookware, jars and more.*

My assistant Teresa transferred a call to me from Attorney Robert Blake in Louden County, NC.

"Hello Attorney Blake, how may I help you?"

"Dana, good morning. I understand you have the capability to reweigh evidence on site in the evidence department, is that correct?"

"Yes. That is correct. I am equipped with certified weights. What is this case all about?" I asked.

"My client, Nick Lumley, had thirteen pounds of Marijuana seized from his residence. Some was in the form of plants. Some was in the form of ready to deliver or smoke, and some was even in a jar of liquid. It appears that they extracted everything he was involved with, including the jar of liquid he had in the oven that may have been a precursor to hashish oil. We need an expert to evaluate the evidence and reweigh everything because anything over ten pounds is trafficking. We are concerned that perhaps the lab weighed the plants to include the root balls and soil."

"Surely, they would know better, or at least I would think. We, of course, need a court order and a time where all those who want to be involved can meet at the evidence location while I reexamine and reweigh. The issue at hand is that now the plants are dry and upon seizure they were not. Upon agreement by all parties, I will do the reweigh and extrapolate the water back in by calculation. Let me know the date and time, and I will clear my calendar."

He responded gratefully.

Approximately two weeks later, I had the order and a date for the event. I was expected to be in Louden County on a Wednesday, and the time was 10:00am.

I had about an hour drive to make in North Carolina's heavy summer rain. So I loaded up and headed out. I arrived slightly early as I normally do and waited only a few minutes before someone came to get me.

We stepped back into a conference room area where some of the evidence was located; the rest was in the basement in boxes and bags that required a hand truck to move.

An evidence custodian and an officer on duty were in the conference room. This was a small county with few resources and a small staff. I asked permission to begin sorting through the boxes brought to the conference room before the attorney who hired me arrived. Permission was granted, and I started with the boxes on the table that contained some dishes, some traces of dried plant material and some empty jars. The second box had three jars sealed with a cap and what appeared to be foil with liquid inside. The liquid was clear for the most part, and the jars were only partially full.

I must have had a look on my face that said: "What the hell is this?"

The officer chimed in, "Those are the jars that were in the oven. We just sealed them up and confiscated them with everything else. It appeared as though he was drying it to extract hashish oil."

"Ah, and was all this weighed as it is, in the jars, with the liquid, and are we certain these jars at some point contained any of the marijuana plant material dried or otherwise?" I asked.

"Yeah, they weighed the whole thing just like you see it, jar and all," the officer told me.

"And, we are all aware that we cannot hold anyone accountable for the cookware and jars containing liquid that we have not proven contains anything illicit or illegal, right?"

I was horrified at what I was hearing! This department was weighing cookware and jars containing fluid to include in with charges of trafficking for Marijuana.

Robert Blake, the defense counsel, arrived, and I filled him in on where we were in the process. I had examined the cookware, the jars with the liquid, and noted that these items should be listed separately perhaps, but not considered as a part of the weight of the trafficking charge.

I am careful not to recommend how or what should be charged That is not my place; however, I can recommend what, perhaps, does not fit in the description of the current charges of trafficking. This may have been a cooking project. He seemed agreeable and took note of what I mentioned.

We were led to an elevator. When the door closed, the custodian said, "It smells really foul down here. Beware." He was not kidding!

When we stepped off the elevator, the very persistent smell of Marijuana hit like a brick wall...Pleasant to some, gagging to others, and for me neutral. I did not like it or dislike it; although I prefer not to be around some of the rotten or skunky smelling stuff. This smell almost had a fruitful nature to it.

We rounded the corner and met the prosecuting attorney and two members of his staff, as well as more officers who wanted to observe. Also, there were two more custodians assisting the first because thirteen pounds was a lot to sort through. This could be a long afternoon depending on how we proceeded. All eyes were on me as the first of many, very large bags of plant material were brought in. I had just unpacked my balance and plugged it in for warming up, and I was putting on my gloves to handle the weights and the evidence. I turned to address my audience of about eight because we all should be on the same page.

"I don't have any real ground rules for operation other than while I am weighing please keep movement to a minimum. Movement in the room can make the balance "jumpy". For the best results, once I am taking a weight, please refrain from walking around me. You are welcome to take photos, notes, or stop me at any time for questions. This process is for everyone, and if I am moving too fast, just let me know.

This evidence was seized while the plants were still alive, and now nearly twelve months later, they are completely dried out. I need for everyone to understand that an extrapolation can be done to approximate the weight when the plant was alive. Marijuana is approximately 70% water. So, I will report the actual weight and then add a 70% water factor back in to determine what the weight at seizure may have been. Also, I will be removing the leaves from the stalks, leaving out the stems, roots and soil from the weight. According to the statute, these items are not smokable and therefore not going to be considered for my purposes.

Additionally, would this team like for me to remove all the plant material from every container, or would we like a representative sample from each bag and extrapolate from there?"

Already we have issues, right? They weighed boxes of cookware, jars with liquid, plants with stalks, stems, roots and soil. They are not likely to argue a representative sample because this will give a range and not be exact. The best the prosecution can hope for is the 70% water weight puts them close to their original number of approximately thirteen pounds. Robert was not going to argue – either way it looks great for his client.

The vote came back for a representation of each large bag, and there were ten. I was there for approximately three hours, most of it down in the smelly evidence area. Bag after bag until we had finished number ten. I removed plant material from several stems from each bag, always careful to get an agreed upon nod from all present on the portions I selected, before weighing the plant material. Then I removed the stems and weighed them separately. Next I placed the material back in the bag from which it came. Upon completion of each bag, I cleaned my balance of residue or plant material from the previous plant (Handy wipes or towelettes work great.). When all the material had been weighed, we were escorted back to the main area.

I headed back to my office, and the report was completed by the end of the following week. Factoring in the water and leaving out the elements not in the statute, we came up with somewhere between two and eight pounds of material seized. That range is based all of the bags and their individual, original weights.

The plant material that is smokable had to be considered for each bag. So if the first bag weighed two pounds and the absolute best scenario is that one plant may yield up to one pound of product, the maximum that this bag could yield was one pound and so by ratios and extrapolations using what we knew to be true, we determined that Mr. Lumley had somewhere between two and eight pounds of smokable product from the plants seized. Either way he was well below the 10 pounds even on the best-case scenario of a one pound yield per plant.

I presented my report and was not called to testify which meant to me the charges were reduced from trafficking to a lesser charge. They had manufacturing and possession for sure but did not have enough for trafficking.

[?]

CHAPTER 4:   *The Condom in the Shoe*

I had a growing interest in criminal DNA testing as did all the rest of the community interested in the "absolute fingerprinting" of a crime scene. I read everything I could get my hands on regarding the subject and was certain I could assist in cases that had DNA as a component of the discovery. I had even gone so far as the take all the tests listed through the "President's Initiative" on DNA testing and reporting. No classes other than the ones offered to the criminal justice world for their scientists existed, and those who were not employed by a state or federal agency could not attend these instructional classes.

The only other option to further my education was via a masters or doctorate in forensic science, but this did not satisfy my desire to learn exactly what the prosecution experts were learning. This was an arena that required defined skills, so I took advantage of every resource I could get and completed virtual analysis on line for instructional purposes. It was the closest I could get to the real thing.

Finally, I got an opportunity to work with DNA. I was already familiar with the attorney because our children played sports together. One Saturday, Rick approached me with his case at a game our children were playing. His client had been in jail for the past three years—awaiting trial on rape that he continued to profess he did not do. He had gone so far to say that the client professed that the condom that was collected out of his shoe, in his apartment was not there before the police entered his room. The seized condom, according to Rick, was covered in dirt and ripped.

Rick said, "It looked like it had been run over by a car." The crime scene was a dirt road in the back of a pickup truck, the gal knew the client, Sam Rutheford. Sam admitted he had had relations with her in the past, but he did not on the evening in question.

Rick concluded: "So with all this that I have mentioned, do you think a DNA test of my client may be the way to go, and is this something you can help with?"

"Absolutely I can help. We need to extract some of his DNA with a cheek swab. We can do this with a sterile Q-tip. After the swab is taken, place the Q-tip in a sealed container, and I will send it off to the lab. The results can take up to six weeks to get back.

Then we need to compare it to the condom – the one they found in his shoe. This will tell us if he was at the scene or not since the condom was supposed to be have been used on the night in question.

Know this though, if it was his condom, while DNA has no time stamp, it does identify if you were present."

"He said the condom is not his. He is insistent about having a DNA test, so I will set it up. We will have to go to the prison and get the sample. Don't wear a skirt and wear long

sleeves...show as little skin as possible. Rules of the prison –
not mine. I will let you know which day we can get in there
to see him. Thanks for agreeing to help."

I was excited and nervous all at once. Finally. A DNA case!
My studying would be put to the test. I was nervous. DNA
has no time stamp! Even if Sam didn't do it and wasn't
there – even if the condom was placed there by someone
other than Sam...Wow! This was something I didn't even
want to think was a possibility.

If it was his, even if it wasn't from that night, or even that
location then he was going to be held accountable for
something he may not have done on that night. So, the
good thing is, this is independent! We don't have to use the
results, but there will be a court order...a paper trail
showing that we requested a test of the condom for DNA.

Surely the prosecution will test it once we are done with our
tests. I was excited at the possibility of setting an innocent

man free...if the results were indeed as Sam said they were going to be – not his DNA.

About a week later, we meet with Sam, and I had to ask him, "Sam was the condom really not yours? Because if it is yours, the DNA will surely prove it."

Sam replied in a soft well-spoken manner with a simple sentence that nearly made me cry. "Mam, please help me get out of here. I did not rape that woman." He had looked me dead in the eye as he spoke, and I was honored that we were working together.

I could not wait until the results were finished and released. This case was going to be a doozy! ,

The condom was released by court order, from the evidence holding department. My sample from Sam was sent independently with instructions to test against the condom that was in route. The sample and instructions were shipped overnight by FedEx with signatures as to not break a chain of custody.

I had a relationship with Marsha, the criminalist, at the lab I used in Pennsylvania and let her know what was on the way. I asked her to call me right away with the results if she could.

The lab was right on time; four weeks later, we had the results. Sam's DNA was NOT on the condom! Holy moly, this means he wasn't at the scene, and he wasn't the perpetrator. Most of all, he was NOT guilty of rape.

I submitted a written report of the laboratory results to Rick. Eventually the charges were dropped, and Sam was released from jail.

He had waited three years for a trial for a crime he did not commit. From the beginning, he had said that the charges were not accurate, that the evidence was not originally in his shoe.

This was an eye opener for me! How in the world could we let this happen? Thank goodness! We have checks and balances. I try not to make too much of what I see, but exactly how did that dirty condom with someone else's DNA end up in Sam's shoe? Why would a condom even be in a shoe in a bedroom when the crime scene was on a dirt road miles from his residence?

I had no definitive answers to the questions in my mind, and the more questions I thought of, the more complicated my thoughts regarding the whole thing became.

Time to shut it down! Turn off my questions, and celebrate the freedom of an innocent man.

⁇

CHAPTER 5: The Perfect DNA Match

On my way home from the office, one of my favorite lawyers called. "What's up, Nick? How are you?"

"Dana, are you still married?"

"Yes, Nick. Nothing has changed in the last week, but thanks for asking. What's up, buddy?"

"Can't blame a guy for trying. Hey, look. I gotta strange case. My guy is in jail for armed robbery. It's him and his brother. They robbed a drug dealer. My guy went in with a bat, and his brother had a gun. There were like four people in the apartment when they crashed in, and there was some fighting. Well, my guy got cut on the hand, and the forensics people got a blood sample at the scene. The results match like perfect. I don't know if there is anything you can help with – a perfect match, man, it's crazy."

I was listening and trying to drive in evening traffic. "Nick, I need to look at the results, and of course, the cases file for collection procedures. Did they do all that stuff right and everything. Do you have the results of the DNA from the lab?" I asked.

"Yeah, I am looking at them now – literally a perfect match. Ughhh, I don't' know...."

I cut him off mid-sentence, "Holy shit, literally a perfect match? That is impossible with that many people in one space; surely some contamination of another party should have been present. Where did they obtain the sample?... like near the floor, up high? Where in the apartment? Was the apartment clean or messy?"

"Dana, ok. The sample was taken from a mirror that was leaning against the wall on the floor."

"There is no way, Nick; no way could they have grabbed a perfect match DNA from a mirror in an apartment where four others reside without picking up some level of contamination. It is almost expected, to some degree, when you have others present. And they were fighting, too. I mean come on. I need to look at the case file. Something really crazy is going on here.

First thing I would like for you to do is ask your guy if they pricked his finger for a blood sample on a swab when they processed him. And also see if they did a cheek swab. Let's start there, and get me the file please."

In disbelief Nick said, "I can't believe you just asked me about the finger prick. My guy has been telling me for weeks they did that, and I thought he was full of shit."

"Well, guess what, buddy. Your client was right, and the science is definitely corroborating his story. The science will tell the truth every time if you let it; forcing it will screw up everything. Looks like we have a screw up here."

Nick didn't even have time to get me the file! He called me only days before the trial because he thought his guy was going down for sure with this perfect match until I told him he may have something. He insisted that I come to court and help him with his cross-examination questions.

I was happy to help. He got a court order rushed and got me added to the witness list for the defense. On my way to the court house, my cell rings. It was Nick.

"Dana, holy shit, you are not going to believe this. The trial is off! Guess what happened! I told them what you said, that they must have somehow presented his reference sample as the evidence. And upon further discovery, the real sample was found in the trunk of the investigator's car!

The sample is no longer valid for testing, something about it being like 100 degrees here lately and degrading and stuff. I don't care. You were right! I gotta run. Talk later."

He hung up before I could get a word in edgewise. Typical

for him, always in a hurry, always talking a mile a minute,

and never forgets to ask if I am still married.

⸮

CHAPTER 6: The 895 Murder Case

Highway 895 was a busy route for commuter traffic to and from work. On a sunny morning, at about 8:30 am, someone called 911 about a body on the side of the road. Right there in plain sight for everyone to notice was a gal that had been stabbed multiple times and left for dead.

It was all over the news, but because I worked like a million hours and was tending to two children and their extracurricular activities – traveling for hockey games and horseback riding, I seemed to miss the news.

Even today, my kids are still absolutely the most important part of my life, but then when they were in their competitive sports (my son playing hockey and my daughter first figure skating, then hockey and finally horseback riding), I didn't want to miss a thing. So I worked my hours such that I could be with them when it was time to travel to the next event.

That meant working long hours Monday thru Thursday; come Friday I was off to the next event with one of the kids. They were never in the same place at the same time so one of us took Mason and the other took Morgan. The next week, we would switch it up. Rarely did we get the opportunity for all of us to be in the same place at the same time, but when we did it was super awesome.

Brand new call, brand new attorney to work with, and we hit if off right away. Billy Turner was his name, and bow ties were his game. He was tall, distinguished looking, and could sing like nobody's business. He had a super full case load; his beautiful wife took care of his books and clerical office work. She sang better than he, according to him. The two of them had a handsome young son whose pictures all over his office told the story...proud dad and loving husband.

The case we were about to embark on was huge...high profile for the area, and we had a full team of consultants. Billy brought me on board from a referral for collection of evidence and DNA results. This was a very complicated case from the very beginning so setting the stage before digging into the evidence was important.

The victim, Shameka Brown, was in her mid 20's and married. She lived on the east side of town and was attending night school on the west side of town at a well-known university. She frequented an apartment where a church bishop and a basketball star at the university she was attending lived. She was attracted to the basketball star and spent many evenings at their place having drinks, watching TV, and hanging out before and after class. The Bishop had a name, but throughout the case, we referred to him as the Bishop. He shall remain so for this story as well. The basketball star's name was Lamont Jackson.

The Bishop owned the residence, and Lamont rented a room from him. The Bishop also had a car that Lamont frequently borrowed. Lamont had no need for a car. The residence was so close to campus that he could walk there, take a bus when needed or simply borrow the Bishop's car.

The Bishop had a day job while his passion remained with the church. His right arm had some neurological damage rendering his right side only partially useful. He adapted his left side for nearly everything, such as opening doors, writing, lifting, etc. People hardly ever noticed because he was so used to doing everything left handed. His right arm appeared perfectly normal except he didn't use it. He had very little grip and nearly no control with his right arm.

Lamont had a passion for swords, knives, and basketball and like everyone else enjoyed having a good time. He had some of his swords on display in cases and seemed to have a fascination with collecting various styles of swords, daggers, and knives.

Shameka was discovered on a Monday morning commute into work at approximately 8:30 am by an observant driver who noticed a body beside the road. The driver called 911 and reported a woman lying lifeless on the side of North Bound 895.

Shameka's husband, Trever Brown, had reported his wife missing because he hasn't seen her in three days. Trever travelled the same highway beside which she was found approximately thirty minutes prior to her being discovered by the concerned citizen.

The Bishop's car was parked on the opposite side of the freeway, headed southbound, and no one was around or in the car. First responders arrived on a gruesome scene where a young girl in her mid 20's had been stabbed multiple times. The fatal wounds, however, appeared to have come from both sides of her neck being sliced open. She was obviously murdered but why, by whom, and what was the killer or killers thinking leaving her in plain sight for everyone to see first thing Monday morning? Officers traced the car back to the Bishop, and they eventually discovered that she frequented the house the Bishop owned.

Detectives quickly went to work on this high-profile case that disturbed so many. A killer on the loose and a brutal murder! This had to be solved.

By the time I was called in to assist on the team, we had a mountain of discovery on our hands that needed to be sorted through. Each of us focused on our area of expertise, and our piles of folders to manage. Mine were the science folders, and of course, I had to look at the collection process at the crime scene.

These folders were not so bad until I got to the photos, they were some of the worst I had ever seen. She had been stabbed approximately 40 times, twice to the neck, cleanly slicing each side. The stab wounds to the torso went completely through her with no bruising or hilt mark on her body. She was small, maybe 135 pounds at best, but still this would take a rather long blade to have gone completely through without leaving any additional marks at the site of puncture.

The investigators collected a pink sweater from the car that reportedly belonged to Shameka. They swabbed DNA from the house and the car. They found her DNA along with the Bishop's and Lamont's. No blood was found in the car; nor was a murder weapon on the scene or in the car. Because the car belonged to the Bishop and Lamont sometimes borrowed it, it seemed reasonable that their DNA would be in the car. Shameka's DNA was also found in the car but in trace amounts consistent with what is known as transfer DNA.

Transfer DNA is where someone leaves a trace of themselves behind on a door knob, for example, and someone else comes behind that person and picks up their DNA and leaves it on a steering wheel, door handle of a car, or some other object. Think of it like muddy feet, one person walks through the mud leaves a heavier trace than someone who walks through their muddy tracks with clean feet. The tracks made by the second person will be lighter because their feet were clean when they stepped in the mud left by the first person.

The Bishop was charged with the crime, and he is the one our team is defending. The husband was removed as a suspect because his alibies checked out. We are not sure what removed Lamont from the list of suspects.

The autopsy revealed that Shameka was approximately eight weeks pregnant at the time of the murder, and it is not clear if she informed either her boyfriend, Lamont, or her husband.

The Bishop had a history of complaints regarding inappropriate behavior with young teen boys, but he was never charged based on the accusations. (A twisted web of information, but what is important to me is the collection of evidence.)

Shameka's DNA was found in the house where Lamont and the Bishop live as well as in the car where they found a sweater that, presumably, belonged to Shameka. A small trace of Shameka's DNA was found in the car, but no blood and no murder weapon. There were no blood wipes or blades taken from the residence where Lamont had his collection. It appears that the Bishop was arrested because it was his car, and he may have had a jealousy issue with Lamont and Shameka. Reportedly, he had a crush on Lamont.

Recap: the Bishop had a bum right arm and owned the car that Lamont sometimes drove. Lamont, the basketball star, and Shameka's boyfriend, owns a knife/sword collection. Shameka is married to Trever and is approximately eight weeks pregnant.

So I start with the DNA and how it was collected and stored because if it wasn't collected properly, there is no need to go any further. Contamination or improper handling renders the sample or samples useless for consideration. The swabs from the house were taken on the counter tops and door knobs and specifically the front door knob on which Shameka's DNA was present. This was no surprise. She was frequented the residence.

The processing of the car included photos. The investigators swabbed the door handles, the inside panels (perhaps looking for traces of blood), and the steering wheel. Everything appeared to have an intact chain of custody, and samples were all processed and stored within the guidelines of good practice and standard industry operating procedures. The DNA on the steering wheel that belonged to Shameka was consistent with transfer DNA.

I presented the report to Billy and the team, and we waited for the trial date. Finally, the date was set, and the court cleared an entire week to get through the trial. We each were prepared with our reports and CV's (Curriculum Vitae) and had been courtroom prepped for cross examination questions. For me, I had some extra prep because a Daubert Hearing was a certainty on this case.

I had never testified on DNA evidence before. I had, of course, worked on some cases, but testifying is slightly different. One side loves you (the defense), and the other side hates you (the prosecutor). Even though I had studied for a few years, I had not run any criminal DNA analysis nor had I worked in a criminal lab before. I was, however, very familiar with reading the data. I consulted with experts in the field, reviewed results multiple times with other experts, and felt there was no time like the present to get the ball rolling. I was nervous but completely confident we were going to do well and that I would get entered in as an expert witness for this trial.

Before going to trial, both sides must disclose everything they intend to present at the trial including the entire witness list, all experts, and consultants along with any reports they have written. This gives both sides an opportunity to prepare cross-examination questions.

It was my intent to opine that transfer DNA levels were not enough to prove Shameka had been in the car that evening. It did, however, mean that whoever was at the wheel of the car very likely picked up her DNA off the front door knob on their way to the car.

A few days prior to the trial, the prosecution found a knife in the car. According to them, it was tucked down in the side of the back seat on the passenger side. Interestingly, they had processed the vehicle twice earlier and did not to find a weapon. Yet on the third time, a few days before trial and six months after the vehicle was found, suddenly a paring knife was found.

A paring knife is normally used to remove the skin from fruits and vegetables and generally has a blade length between four and seven inches. There was no time to swab for DNA. Because of the passage of time and the elevated temperatures at the time of the murder, degradation surely would be a factor, so this was a moot point. But, we now had a "murder weapon" according to the prosecution.

I may seem skeptical, but who wouldn't be at this point? And if you review the photos and the stab wounds, anyone could see that the blade they were about to present in the courtroom would not have been consistent with the wounds on Shameka's body.

This is not my area though; only the DNA is within my purview. I could only hope that the blade would be recognized for what it was—just a blade. Perhaps someone would ask where the evidence is that traces it back to the crime scene. Fingerprints, blood, something?

What a thing to deal with this close to the trial, and a continuance was denied. So carry on soldiers, we have a trial to attend.

The week of the trial was finally upon us. It's fall moving into winter, so wearing a suit is not so bad this time of year. My day usually comes later in the week, but I'm on call every day the trial is in session. The first day is generally "pick the jury day". The second and third days are usually when the prosecution gets heard, sometimes they take longer depending on how much evidence they have to enter into the record and experts to question.

My day came on Thursday, and I was ready. Of course, we started out with a Daubert Hearing for the judge to determine if there was enough evidence for me to be tendered in as an expert in the field of forensic chemistry and DNA review. Success it was after about an hour! The judge rendered me an expert. A Daubert Hearing takes place outside of the jury's presence, and once the judge rendered me an expert, the jury came back in, and we went through it all over again for the jury.

For my presentation, I had a flip chart demonstrating to the jury the difference between transfer DNA and DNA left by the actual donor. Thirteen points of reference can be determined for the donor. A low level DNA result may only show ten of the thirteen points and may have a very faint resolution.

This was the circumstance we had with Shameka's DNA on the steering wheel. We got the DNA removed from being considered due to the transfer or low levels and the fact that she frequented the residence anyway. So this had nothing to do with the Bishop's guilt or innocence. After successfully eliminating the DNA evidence from consideration, my task was completed. I was dismissed from the courtroom.

Billy called me a few days later and filled me in on the outcome of the trial. The jury convicted the Bishop. During the presentation of the evidence, and particularly the knife, they had an expert on their team who testified that it was certainly possible for a paring knife to penetrate through without leaving hilt marks or bruising form the knife if you depressed the chest and/or torso with your other hand while stabbing.

Let us not forget the neurological damage to the Bishop's right arm. That damage made the outcome of this trial unbelievable! Who actually killed Shameka Brown? Who knows? It was clear to most, although apparently not the jury, that it was not likely the Bishop! Yet, he is now serving life in prison for the murder of Shameka Brown.

CHAPTER 7: Sexual Assault or Accidental Transfer?

DNA can be the best thing ever or the worst thing ever; it depends on the circumstances. It has no time stamp, and some levels of DNA are can linger on surfaces for years, based on the storage locations and temperatures. This makes it a powerful tool for solving previously unsolvable crimes – even many years after the fact.

DNA has proven the innocence of those who were wrongfully convicted. Peter Neufeld and Barry Scheck, founders of the Innocence Project in 1992, have been using DNA to do just that. As of July of 2017, 351 cases had been cleared.

DNA is everywhere you are, and you can leave traces of yourself just by breathing in a room or touching the countertops, walls, door knobs, etc. So, if the parents of a small child engage in intercourse and the frightened child later climbs into bed because of a storm or to watch some late night or early morning TV perhaps, semen may collect on the child's clothing. Believe it or not, there have been studies where DNA from semen was transferred in the washing machine and stayed present for identification even after several washings.

The next case was such a cased! And it also taught me to disclose only the fact or facts I intended to opine and not the lengthy explanation of the process I used to arrive at my conclusions. Being too wordy in my reports likely cost me the opportunity to testify in this next case, or perhaps it was a call from an assistant district attorney from anther county who wasn't very fond of my work.

The case involved a 10-year old girl whose parents were not getting along and had started discussing a possible separation. The mother accused the father of sexually assaulting the daughter and requested DNA testing of the child's panties. I was brought into the case late and spent several hours preparing a lengthy report which I later realized may have been a bad idea. Short and sweet is much better and would have allowed me more sleep.

The courthouse was several hours from my office, so I started early in the morning start to get there by 10 am per the request of the attorney. My report had been turned over a few days earlier to be a part of the defense discovery and to be allowed in for the jury to consider.

I started my report with what was not present. There was no DNA found on the child, no bruising, no tearing, no blood, no physical sign consistent with penetration but more importantly no DNA on the child and only trace levels on the panties. The child did spend time in the marital bed watching TV, and the parents were still engaging in sexual intercourse.

I presented the opinion that the DNA found on the child's panties was most likely a result of sitting on the bed in the area where sex intercourse had taken place. I cited many studies where similar levels of DNA were found under similar circumstances and even in some cases had been transferred in the laundry.

The attorney waited until I got to the courthouse to fill me in. The judge had every intention of disqualifying me as a witness because I had not had the same training as the crime lab analyst. Therefore, according to the judge, because I lacked the same training that was provided to the crime lab analyst, I was not qualified to testify on the evidence. Yet, none of this training was available to anyone not employed by the state or federal agencies that provided the training.

My outside training and studies did not matter to this judge. Nor did the numerous studies I had cited. I was disappointed that I would be disqualified without even a

Daubert Hearing. I couldn't imagine a decision being rendered in a case before all the evidence was considered.

I was not going to enter the courtroom. It was the second time I had been disqualified for sexual assault DNA. This was inconceivable after having been entered in as an expert on transfer DNA in a high-profile murder case. The assistant district attorney for this case had gotten a call from the assistant district attorney (DA) of a more controversial case that I had just worked and been disqualified from testifying. Based on an exchange between two assistant DAs, the judge disqualified me before I even had an opportunity to present my qualifications or the evidence. So I went from a high profile murder trial with DNA to disqualified on a case of sexual assault. Interesting scenario, but not enough to make me give up.

Gunshot wounds are not my thing, and I am not qualified to be an expert in the field. That is something best left for medical examiners. But where are those for the defense team?

This was a classic gang related crime – one side fighting with the other side about whatever they fight about. Next thing you know weapons are brandished, shots are fired, and low and behold, someone gets hurt or worse.

Late one Friday night going into early Saturday morning, the tempers flared at a summer gathering of gang members when a rival gang showed up. The mood went from casual partying to posturing with threats. Things went from bad to worse as the guns came out. Shots were fired... multiple rounds from multiple caliber pistols, from both sides of the street.

As the sirens grew louder and closer, those who could, scattered. One of the gang leaders, Tyrone Williams, lay on the ground with a hole in the middle of his torso. He was not breathing! His best friend hovered over him, yelling at him, yelling out in pain, and crying uncontrollably. Tyron had been caught in the crossfire.

On the scene, everyone was quick to start throwing blame...where they thought the fatal shot came from, who released the bullet, etc. Collectively, the witnesses said the fatal shot came from across the street and most likely from Wendell Johnsons' gun. As he left the scene, Wendell had tossed the 9mm Smith & Wesson into the ditch. The weapon did not belong to him, was not registered to him, and he wasn't worried about it being traced back to him. It took a few days before investigators caught up with Wendell. By then, they had a warrant for his arrest. The fatal shot had come from a 9mm bullet. Although it appeared that they had the murder weapon, no further testing was done on the weapon to see if the round that killed Tyrone had come from Wendell's gun.

After all, this was a "gang thang"! If they were' getting one off the street by death and the other by conviction, what did they need to worry about? Two down at once might look like a great score. But, what about the investigation? Did the weapon they had really fire the fatal shot? Did the partial prints found on the weapon that belonged to Wendell really mean that he fired the fatal shot? Many rounds from many weapons were fired that evening, and likely more than one 9mm was at the scene.

I was asked to review the case files. Initially, I was hesitant. Gunshot wounds were not on my "scope". After several moments of almost begging by the attorney, I agreed.

This was a gang related incident and no one wanted to be a part of it. No matter how you slice it, nobody wins. The witnesses suddenly get amnesia. Anybody in the area who is familiar with the gang members are afraid to talk, and most people outside of the area won't get involved because, distant or not, gang connections are everywhere. No one knows where they are or where they end. It's a messy tangled web that no one wants to get caught in.

So why should I take the case? No one else will. Yet everyone deserves a fair trial in the United States of America. (Go me, and my "deliver the real truth" attitude).

The attorney, George Lightfoot, was apologetic for the "light" discovery file of the incident and the investigation notes. The file included eye witness accounts of the night in question and a few poorly done hand drawings of the scene with possible trajectory points that strangely seemed to match the eye witness accounts of the incident. There was also a file detailing the collection of the evidence which included items listed with the chain of custody intact.

Among the items collected was the 9mm Smith & Wesson semi-automatic pistol presumed to be the murder weapon and a few shell casings. All that gun fire and only a handful of shell casings were found? Seems like more and more folks are carrying revolvers nowadays I though. Fewer rounds but less metal left behind.

The photos of Tyrone's wounds from the medical examiner's report showed he had been hit a couple of times. According to the medical examiner, the fatal wound was to the chest. The thing that caught my eye, however, was what was not included – trajectory of any of the shell casings, blood splatter, or other tools of the trade that may have indicated pathway of the bullets fired.

I noticed that the chest wound was surrounded by tiny burn marks known as stippling. Stippling is the creation of a pattern simulating varying degrees of solidity or shading by using small dots. Tyrone had on a cotton polyester blend shirt on the evening he was fatally shot. Due to the loss of blood at the wound site, it would not have been easy to detect burn marks in or around his wound on the night of the incident. Besides, it was dark outside. After he was more closely examined, however, the burn marks would have been more apparent.

A dark almost solid burn pattern surrounded by a broader stippling pattern was apparent. Most likely, the solid burn pattern came from his polyester blend shirt. Polyester melts at low heat temperatures and becomes almost liquefied at slightly higher temperatures, depending on the content of the blend. Even to a non-expert like me, the amount of burn and stippling at the wound site made it apparent that the fatal shot came at close range.

"Wait a minute," I thought. "What did the medical examiners' notes say about the distance of the shot? Surely they would have noted it, then we wouldn't need an expert on gunshot wounds."

Examining the notes more closely, however, showed that the notes seemed to be consistent with the eye witness accounts of the incident!

"Damn it, how could this be possible? Surely the medical examiner knows the difference here – even my untrained eye can plainly see this wound did not occur from 20-25 feet away as reported!"

I began looking for an expert we could pull in because I was not likely to get tendered in as an expert outside of my "wheel house". Nothing! No one had the time or was available or was willing to jump in. Looks like I have to go with the mountain of documentation and pictures for reference and pray the judge tenders me in. Otherwise, this guy is toast. According to what is in his case file, he will likely get convicted for a murder he did not commit.

Trial day arrived, and with it, another three-hour early morning departure to get to the courthouse on time. This seems to be a regular thing now; I'm a road warrior for the truth in justice. The drive was nerve racking because this was not my "wheel house". Yet, this guy deserved representation, and I'll give it my best.

I arrived at the courthouse; all discovery had been disclosed. The prosecution had my report stating that the fatal wound could not have occurred from 20-25 feet away due to the stippling around the wound. We are still going to trial, and I am still scheduled to testify.

After the prosecution team rested from entering evidence and witness testimony, it was time for the defense team to call witnesses. A Daubert Hearing to establish expert witness status before calling other defense witnesses is the norm. I almost always go on the stand last, and this time wasn't any different. The judge excused the jury, and the defense counsel and the prosecution began the questioning to establish my credentials.

Success! I was entered in as a forensic scientist, but not a gunshot wound expert which is great. I can still speak generally about the wound being from close range because of the stippling, but nothing else. GREAT NEWS, it's all I need to discuss in addition to the effort or lack thereof of the crime scene notes and processing of the crime scene.

My testimony was a game changer for Wendell. There may have been things he was guilty of, but murder in this incident was not one of them. Later, the police discovered that the bullet that killed Tyrone came from his best friend's gun. Tyrone turned around right into his line of fire during the shooting.

CHAPTER 9: Meth in the Mountains

Because I had done a reweigh case in the mountains of West Virginia with Attorney Carl Wright, he referred me to Attorney James Cartwright. Attorney Cartwright was working a federal case that involved three men convicted of manufacturing methamphetamine in an open outdoor arena known as a national park. It was the sentencing hearing that was of interest now.

Because the operation took place in a national park, a protected area, some additional work was necessary to determine what, if any hazards may have been created and/or left behind when the manufacturing operation was discontinued, broken down, and disposed of. Another important factor was the local sheriff's claim that he suffered upper respiratory issues that began after the arrest of the three men and the breakdown of the outdoor lab. The sheriff's claim was based on his efforts during the initial arrest and the fact that the lab was fully active when he approached the scene.

James explained that my task was to determine if any threat to life – human, animal, plant or to the soil, or water. I needed to explain any level of threat or toxicity present at any time throughout the manufacturing process or at the time of the arrests. The sheriff's claim of injury or respiratory damage was based on his inhalation of the toxic fumes from the active lab.

I agreed to take the case. No pressure. Right? Three guys were awaiting sentencing, and my testimony of the dangers of their manufacturing process was a key component to determine how long they would spend in federal prison. And, as an aside, don't forget the sheriff! Who risks his life day in and day out to maintain the safety of his county. Now he has respiratory issues after entering a hot lab zone where methamphetamine was being manufactured. Holy cow, my work is cut out for me on this one. Lots of references will be needed for this report. My I's are always dotted, and T's crossed every time, but the references would be the important credibility builder. If I choose the wrong references, it might negate my report and therefore my testimony.

I waited for the detailed file to come in. I had requested the collection of all notes and evidence logs about the lab site and the notes regarding the size of the batches prepared over the course of the nearly two-year manufacturing run the guys had. I prepared a detailed report based on a 46% theoretical yield from the United States Sentencing Commission's Amendment 611. The 192 pills or 30 milligrams of pseudoephedrine would yield only an estimated 2.65 grams of Methamphetamine Hydrochloride.

Records indicated previous purchases of 30 milligrams of pseudoephedrine pills totaling approximately 75 grams in weight. The active ingredient in pseudoephedrine pills can range from 5% to 70% of the actual pill weight, so the yield may have been somewhere between 1.71 grams and 24.04 grams of Methamphetamine Hydrochloride based on the estimated 46% mentioned earlier.

The night the sheriff entered the area of the active lab, 192 pills were at the location. Starting with the referenced calculations and the possible threat to human life, I built the foundation for my calculations in three areas: threat to human life, threat to the soil, and threat to the water shed. While the toxicity comes from the ammonia released during the manufacturing process, other dangers are present like fires and explosions. We, however, were mostly concerned with waste from the process, environmental hazards in the immediate area, and the threat to human life.

The manufacturing of Methamphetamine Hydrochloride requires two gallons of ammonia per pound of finished product. Each lab and each chemist, backyard or otherwise, may have a different yield based on individual practices. For this case, however, we are basing everything on the 46%

theoretical yield listed in Amendment 611. So 192 pills

equals 5.76 grams of pseudoephedrine and requires 59.43

grams of ammonia to produce Methamphetamine

Hydrochloride with 52.27 parts per million (ppm) of

ammonia being released and present during the first 10

minutes of release. The hazard level is 150 ppm as reported

by the US Department of Justice Office of Community

Oriented Policing Service (DOJ COPS) from their assessment

of Clandestine Laboratory Clean Up. The results were clear,

and the data was supported by Environmental Protection

Agency (EPA) and Area Locations of Hazardous

Atmospheres (ALHOA).

The amount of waste in this case was minimal. No threat to

the soil could be determined, and the water shed was

significantly further away. Consequently, if no threat existed

to the soil, then clearly there would be no run off into the

water. The threat of harm from the ammonia or waste from

the process to humans, animals, and/or plants seemed not to be an issue.

As for the sheriff who claimed respiratory issues, those may be real. Hypersensitivity to ammonia may have triggered something within him, but it was neither within my expertise nor my place to determine the sheriff's health status. I could not say if he was affected or not. My job was to describe, from a scientific point of view, the danger presented by the ammonia and/or the waste from the manufacturing process to life that existed in the area on the night when the manufacturing operation was discontinued, broken down, and disposed of.

I knew I had done a good job on my written report and oral testimony when the prosecution crossed with a question: "Ms. Way, could a bird have been injured if he swooped down to pick up a piece of the fertilizer?"

I waited for the objection, then the sustained remark from the judge before I answered, "I wasn't asked to evaluate birds flying in to pick up pieces of the fertilizer, so I cannot comment on the risk to the birds at this point."

The sentencing was adjusted to the standard for manufacturing methamphetamine in an open outdoor arena known as a national park without the extra five years for posing a threat to life – human, animal, plant or to the soil, or water.

CHAPTER 10: *Your DNA Can End Up Anywhere*

A gay couple and their mothers lived in a quiet neighborhood in south Louisiana. Philip and Marco were taking care of their mothers who had grown more dependent as they attempted to live on their social security checks each month.

The sons and their mothers had been in the neighborhood only a few years when new neighbors moved in. They seemed nice enough, friendly in passing anyway. The neighbors had one son, Trey, who was in his early teens. Even though it was summer and the school year had not yet started, the move was tough on the teenager.

They lived in harmony until Trey's dad, a former Marine, began to pick up on Philip and Marco's relationship. He was not gay friendly and acted as if the situation was a contagious threat. Trey, on the other hand, had become friends with them and took an even more special liking to

Marco. He was a typical teen who had moved from place to place with a military family, had few friends, didn't get too attached, and stayed ready to move again. This time was slightly different; Trey's dad was retired and they were settling in for a more permanent situation.

Trey had a basketball net out front and played regularly. Marco, a traveling sales rep, joined him when his afternoons were free. Even though Marco had a home office, he spent approximately 60% of his work time travelling. When he was home, he liked to catch up on his cardio and weight training. Over the course of the next year, Trey and Marco developed a workout schedule together. As their relationship grew, Marco offered to help him with his computer skills.

On a warm summer night while Marco's mom was out of town, the guys decided to have relations in her room. Her room was on the other side of the house and seemed more private than their room right next door to Philip's mom.

Neither Phillip nor Marco was aware that Trey was lurking outside his bathroom window with a direct view of them. He watched until they climaxed; then he ran around and knocked on the sliding glass door of the bedroom, perhaps hoping to be next. Somewhere between the basketball and computer lessons, Trey assumed that what he felt for Marco was mutual. Yet, Marco was as surprised as Philip when he noticed Trey at the door.

Trey, wearing only a pair of shorts, had a white t-shirt wrapped around his neck. He made it appear that he was welcome and was looking to partake. Marco tried his best to explain that he did not mean to lead him in this manner and that they would never be any more than friends because he was in a relationship with Philip.

Trey went from eager to get into a three-way relationship where Philip shared Marco to dangerously angry when he was denied. Philip left the room too upset to continue to listen to Trey. Marco convinced him to leave before his father realized where he was and went to console Philip. Trey was left alone briefly before leaving the residence.

When the two went back to straighten up the room and clean up the remnants of their sexual encounter, they noticed the condom Marco had on was missing. Marco swore he dropped it on the floor as he quickly tried to put on pants when he noticed Trey at the door. Philip thought he might have thrown it in the trash; either way the room was now clean. They now also knew this room had a clear view from the fence that separated their house form Trey's.

A few days later, an officer of the law knocked on the door and requested a voluntary DNA reference sample from Marco who had been accused of sexually assaulting Trey. The men felt like a steam roller had just come in and demolished everything. No real words could explain the rush of emotions that went through the whole house. Marco had not sexually assaulted Trey, so he felt confident all would end well.

Philip, on the other hand, had contacted an attorney – just in case. Turns out Philip had made the right move!

Trey had a rape kit done the afternoon after the supposed sexual encounter and hence the reason for the reference sample.

Several months into the case and the discovery, Philip reached out to me by phone. The elements of the case were:

1.   Marco was accused of not just one sexual assault, but multiple sexual assaults on different occasions.

2.   Dates on which Marco was accused of performing said assaults were also dates he was out of town for work with receipts to accompany the dates in question.

3.   The rape kit was only done on Trey. The notes indicated that Trey had defecated and showered prior to arrival at the clinic.

4.   A nearly perfect match sample, crystal clear, of Marco's DNA was discovered in Trey's anus.

5.   Marco's condom was missing from the room where he had sex with Philip.

6.   Trey had threatened Marco, claiming he would regret his decision to deny him sex.

7.   There was no collection or swabbing of Marco's body because he had showered, rendering gaining a sample useless.

8.   None of Marco's clothes were gathered as evidence.

This seemed like a case with holes everywhere. I was more than willing to join the team. Phillip and I had agreed to my normal fees that excluded the countless hours of phone time. The charges are for my report and the necessary research.

I was astounded when I got the call that the attorney had decided to go in without an expert witness. All the work I had done was for nothing, and without representation on the defense side, it was likely the outcome would not fare well for Marco.

Marco was found guilty and sentenced to fifteen years for lewd and lascivious conduct. Philip was beside himself and began working to get Marco's conviction overturned. I stayed involved even at the post-conviction level.

At the hearing requesting a new trial and deeming his first attorney ineffective, the new attorney decided to pull out because we had no new evidence to support requesting a new trial. He offered Philip an opportunity to charge him with ineffective counsel and stated that his best option would be to find new evidence so that we could gain a new trial.

Yet, the jury didn't hear (1) about the dates Trey accused

Marco of having relations with him when Marco was out of

town, (2) that retrieving a DNA sample after more than 12

hours, especially after showering and defecating may be

difficult, and the DNA less than pristine, and (4) that the

missing condom was full of Marco's sperm from his

encounter with Phillip.

Marco is serving his 15-year sentence, and not a day goes

by that I don't have him and Philip in my thoughts.

Cocaine testing in hair has become a staple for many factories and industries where the job itself is hazardous, and even more so when one is under the influence the drug. Companies take it seriously enough to test randomly for drugs in both urine and hair. Hair is known for being able to determine historical usage while urine has as small as a 24 hour window for some illicit substances.

Mr. Swarez had worked for a major oil refinery as a welder for more than 10 years and had never had a positive urine or hair test until November of 2014. The refinery hired a subcontractor with a mobile collection unit to collect hair and urine specimens on site. Jose Swarez and about twenty others were called to the collection trailer shortly after arriving at work.

Jose went through the motions as usual. On this occasion, however, things seemed a bit disorganized with multiple people in a small confined space. Samples were not being sealed before another one was taken. Gloves were not changed after each sample was taken, and the scissors used to collect the hair were not wiped between subjects. Jose had not been through this type of collection before, but he assumed he still had nothing to worry about. After all, he was clean, and the results should be the same as always, clean. He returned to work and thought nothing more about it.

However, approximately a week after the onsite testing, Jose was called to the Human Resources Department and handed a termination letter stating that cocaine was found in his hair. Not only did he lose his current job, but he is now flagged in the specialized database of talent indicating that he tested positive for cocaine. He is off limits to anyone needing his trade skills. No one will hire a welder who uses cocaine!

Jose's attorney, Sarah Grant, asked me to be part of her team. She provided me a data file and collection paperwork. We built a team to fight the oil refinery, the lab, and the offsite collection facility. Our team was also armed with a toxicologist to help explain how one might have a negative urine result with a positive hair sample. Historically, Jose had not engaged in illicit activity. So how does one explain all of this?

Hair testing is great for historical data, but hair is highly prone to external contamination. Cocaine is a fine powder, and to create a known standard for comparison, the lab may have had to prepared one with the fine powder. It is also possible that the sample was contaminated prior to the lab receiving it. Or, in the haste to package it, the sample may have gotten mixed-matched with another name. According to Jose, neither the scissors nor the gloves were changed during the collection process, so a transfer could have been taken place there also.

Jose and his family lost almost all their possessions while he was unable to work in his specialty trade. The money he did make was only a third of what he had made at the refinery. The case, deliberations, and depositions leading up to the trail took more than a year.

Finally, the day of the trial arrived, and Jose's team had "a smoking gun", a sample swap was discovered at the lab. Placement into the instrument autosampler was the source of the sample mix-up.

It took more than a year, but Jose and his family prevailed. They were paid a fee for the sample mix-up, and case after case has come into Sarah Grant's office.

?

Manny was the Cocaine king of the small town, and because he was great at delegating, he had avoided the clutches of law enforcement for more than a decade. The young girl who lived next door, Veronica, frequented Manny's house when his nephew, Rodney, was in town. Rodney visited on weekends mostly until school was out, then most of the summer he spent with his uncle.

Veronica was adopted by the Henderson family when she was only a few months old. She was a free-spirited character who seemed to thrive on attention from her elders. Steve Henderson was a TV Evangelist and Sheila Henderson, a warm and loving housewife who supported the foundation of her husband's career and raised their daughter.

The summer of 2010 was starting just like the others when Rodney showed up to be with Uncle Manny. Veronica had been doing some light cleaning for Manny and sometimes joined him for a meal afterward. Veronica and Rodney went on their traditional trail walk the first night he was in town and spent the evening catching up from last summer. As the summer progressed, Veronica was spending more and more time over at Manny's. She had become so comfortable there that she was asking for money, and Manny had no problem tossing her $5 every now and then. After all, she was doing some housework for him.

Veronica was only 14 years old. While she was spending time with Rodney, she loved the attention she was getting from Manny. In some ways, she was kind of playing house with Manny, taking care of the house work and having dinner with him sometimes. Manny had started to see that she was spending a little too much time at his place, and when she asked him for money, he denied her this time. He was trying to slowly let her know she needed to spend less time at his house and more time at hers.

She became emotional when he denied her money claiming he owed her for everything she did for him. She started throwing punches at him, and during the tussle, the curtains came down from the window behind the couch. She eventually gave in and left the house claiming he would regret not paying her.

That afternoon, the local law enforcement sought to question Manny. As he walked down the street, headed back to his house, he was approached and arrested for statutory rape. Veronica was at the hospital having a rape kit done. Manny was processed and placed in jail to await proceedings.

Attorney Gordon Riley from the public defender's office was assigned to his case. Gordon contacted me to see if I was interested in being a part of the defense team. He sent the discovery package to see if there was anything I thought I could do for Manny and the case.

First thing I did was request the evidence from Manny's clothing, that seemed to be missing from the package. The only testing they did on Manny was a buccal reference swab (cheek swab). Interesting because the incident happened in the same day and if there was penetration as Veronica said, then he clearly would have traces of her on him. Yet, they did not confiscate his clothing for testing.

I was told that he showered and changed his clothes. Besides the results from him did not matter so long as what they found on her was a match for him. They did indeed find a match, but, the match was not entirely conclusive for Manny, only eight of the thirteen loci that they look for were a match. So, this means that more than one person may have had sex with Veronica or a family member's DNA was present and not Manny's.

My report was very detailed and had supporting documentation regarding familial DNA and noted that if Rodney, Manny's nephew, had been spending time with her might it not be possible that he left the DNA behind? What the judge thought might be a slam dunk case to get a well know cocaine dealer off the streets suddenly had holes in it.

The investigators looked a little lazy for not following through with every possible angle of this tangled web. The state was getting ready to look less than stellar, and I had the key. The worst thing I did was state how I obtained my opinion: the results were inconclusive and supporting evidence was lacking. Saying too much cost me a qualification,

The judge ordered a Daubert Hearing, and even though I had been entered in as an expert on DNA science in another courtroom, this judge was not going to allow me to testify in her courtroom. She disqualified me on the basis that I had not had the exact same training as the state lab employees.

Unbelievable! I am not eligible for this training. Nor is anyone else who is not employed by the state crime laboratory.

What is one to do? Walk out of the courtroom and regroup? But where to from here?

I asked the family to keep me informed of Manny's status and to please contact me if there was anything further I could do. I promised them that I would offer my services at no charge if I could help.

Manny was convicted and sentenced to twenty years for statutory rape. Over the next seven years, the family as well as Manny kept in touch with me, and now The Innocence Project has his case. His attorney should be charged with ineffective counsel for not requesting a reference swab from Rodney, and the judge should be dismissed.

She did what she had to do to get a drug dealer off the streets by convicting him of a crime he most likely did not commit. Her disqualification kept me from testifying in, at least 1 more case, in that state.

I learned to keep my reports to facts and references only and to present how I arrived at them in the courtroom before the jury. Additionally, I will no longer work with a few attorneys.

CHAPTER 13:   *Trust and Verify*

I always had faith in the system until I observed the corruption first hand. Why in the world is this even a case? What is so wrong with this system that you must not only keep yourself out of trouble, but pray that no one accuses you of a crime either?

People are not incapable of making mistakes, and some of us are less than honest. Unfortunately, sometimes an employee's actions are directed by those above them within the system. I have witnessed actions that are completely mind blowing and can find no rationalization for them. Cases listed in this book are just such examples. The breakdown in the system may be due to selfish satisfaction for the participants providing the proof of guilt and the weaknesses of the system combined with the laziness of the defenders of the accused.

Not all of this can be seen as malicious; sometimes when we hear a story presented, we lean towards the same side as the story teller. It is not until we hear the other side of the story that we may change our minds. This indicates a need to be aware of all the facts before we form an opinion. We need all the "puzzle pieces" before we align with those who present "evidence" for either side – prosecutor or defense.

Investigators working a crime scene are supposed to remain neutral and un-opinionated until all the pieces are present to determine the most accurate picture of the crime committed. Unfortunately, some seem to – in the interest of saving time – create the picture all too quickly. Then they feel the need to continue to seek parts that fit where they believe the guilt lies.

This is the wrong approach to solving any crime, but it happens all the time. Investigators team up with state or federal government attorneys and gather what they need to present in court to continue to provide validation for their chosen scenario. This may or may not be an accurate picture of what happened.

In other cases, there may a perceived opportunity to increase assets or revenue for the law enforcement office or department. So sometimes a reported value close to a trafficking charge may be embellished to place a problem citizen in prison longer and/or to gain some additional resources for the arresting body of that state or government entity. This can be done because there are few who can verify or disprove what is being presented by the state or government agency. For years, and even today, it is rare to see experts on a defense council bench in court. Most defendants cannot afford an expert witness or the attorney assigned will not file for a court appointed expert.

Some experts will not work court appointed cases. The state and the federal government already have their experts on the payroll. The burden is on the defendant to provide funds for his or her expert witness. If the appointed attorney does not feel the need to have an expert or any level of verification of the evidence even if the defendant feels it necessary, the defendant is stuck, generally having to do without because they lack the funds to pay expert witnesses.

As in the case with Manny, there was more than one person's DNA present in the vaginal swab. The DNA that was discovered was not an exact match, and I was disqualified from testifying before the jury. It was not because I didn't know what I was doing. On the contrary, I was getting ready to point out that critical pieces of the puzzle that may have led to his innocent verdict were being left out.

The judge wanted Manny off the street and found a way to get what she wanted. In the case of the bishop, I am convinced that the real murderer is still at large unless they arrested him or her on a different crime and got a conviction. The saddest part is that more than one person is affected when an innocent person is incarcerated, and the guilty party sometimes is allowed to walk freely.

I don't think most people set out to frame, plant, or adjust any statement or piece of evidence. I think it happens as a result of not slowing down to take the time to work each case with an open mind and with full integrity from the top to bottom of the system. Taking the time to let the science tell the story and not using the science to verify what we think is the true story is most likely the root cause in many wrongful accusations, arrests, and convictions.

We live in a fast paced world of technology, we need to bring ourselves back to the basics, refresh our thought processes, and analyze and deduce from the pieces we have in place. We need to quit trying to put the round peg in the square hole. it really doesn't fit, but many lives are impacted by the lack of integrity in investigations.

My advice for defendants – trust only with verification. It never hurts to get a second opinion of what your situation looks like. If you had to have brain surgery, would you trust the outcome to only one surgeon?

www.ingramcontent.com/pod-product-compliance
Lightning Source LLC
Chambersburg PA
CBHW060617210326
41520CB00010B/1375